Concise Guide to Customs of Minority Ethnic Religions

D1355153

CONCISE GUIDE TO

Customs of Minority Ethnic Religions

David Collins
Manju Tank
Abdul Basith

arena

Published by
Arena
Ashgate Publishing Limited
Gower House
Croft Road
Aldershot
Hants GU11 3HR
England

Ashgate Publishing Company
Old Post Road
Brookfield
Vermont 05036

British Library Cataloguing in Publication Data

Concise Guide to Customs of
Minority Ethnic Religions
  I. Collins, David
  291

ISBN 1 85742 120 5

Typeset in Century Old Style by Bournemouth Colour
Graphics, Parkstone, Dorset and printed in Great Britain
by Loader Jackson, Arlesey

Contents

About the Authors

David Collins M.A., B.Sc. (Econ.) Hons., Dip.S.W. is Development Officer of Portsmouth Diocesan Council for Social Responsibility. The council has a special interest in social justice issues – hence its participation in the creation of this guide.

Manju Tank J.P. was formerly Senior Community Liaison Officer with Hampshire County Council Education Department. She is currently reading part-time for a Masters degree in Politics (Equal Opportunities) at Southampton University.

Abdul Basith M.A. was formerly a Community Liaison Officer with Hampshire County Council Education Department.

Foreword

'Religion has been a rock upon which the British people have built their hopes and cast their cares'. When Sir Winston Churchill wrote these words, most people in Britain would have called themselves Christians whether or not they were churchgoers.

The influence of the Christian gospel has been all-pervading in forming the culture and customs of our society. We take for granted much Christian tradition, both in our attitudes and routines of daily life.

Yet, in a comparatively short time, we have become a plural society. There are significant groups of people whose culture and religion are not founded on Christianity. They have the right to respect and freedom for expression of their traditional culture and religious beliefs.

Often, these are not known or understood by others. This guide has been produced to heighten sensitivity in the wider community, and so enable all to participate fully in the life of this nation. It is to be warmly welcomed.

The Anglican Bishop of Portsmouth
The Right Reverend Timothy J. Bavin M.A.

Acknowledgements

We would like to thank the following people for their help in the preparation of the guide: Rev. Anthony Dee (Minister of the Portsmouth and Southsea Hebrew Congregation), Kirpan Singh Digpal (President of the Portsmouth Gurdwara), Manchi Geddes, Ho Tran (Resettlement Officer, the Ockendon Venture), Ijahnya Christian (Anguilla, Eastern Caribbean), Roland and Cam Tu Dowling, Raj Singh Panesar, Chui Fai Fong, Lai Pik Wun, Protima Tadevossian, and many members of the minority ethnic communities of Hampshire.

The comments of staff of the Hampshire County Council Education and Social Services Departments, Hampshire Careers Service, H.M. Prison, Kingston, Portsmouth and South East Hampshire Health Authority, and Southampton and South-West Hampshire Health Authority were also valuable in the production of the guide. David Collins' post is funded by Hampshire Social Services.

While we are grateful for this help and encouragement, responsibility for the contents of the guide remains with the authors.

Introduction

The purpose of this guide, as the foreword suggests, is to raise awareness, create sensitivity, and promote equality of opportunity. Rather than claiming to provide all the answers. It draws attention to matters where sensitive enquiry is needed.

It outlines religious rules, and indicates a range of individual choice in the extent to which these are adhered to. Custom and practice vary widely. Some Muslim girls cover their heads; others do not. Some Sikh parents insist upon their school-age daughters wearing Shalwar (loose-fitting trousers), while others do not. These are typical examples of the extent of variation. You cannot rely on standard assumption; always ask what practice is preferred.

As with majority ethnic groups, it should not be assumed that all members of minority ethnic groups are necessarily practising religious believers. However, as with the majority, their beliefs will have powerfully influenced their family and social traditions and attitudes.

In the field in which we are working, there is a vast range of information. This may be approached in many different ways, of which ours is but one. The information we have decided to present has been selected partly because of circumstances in Hampshire, from which the guide originated, and partly from a desire to reach what is likely to be an audience predominantly from a Christian culture, even if they are not churchgoers.

We recognize the substantial numbers of Christians of various denominations found among minority ethnic groups. But we have chosen to describe customs and beliefs that are not Christian in origin, about which we feel much needs to be learnt, if the needs of their adherents are to be respected.

General Notes

The Race Relations Act (1976)
The Act defines what is lawful and unlawful in the treatment of members of minority ethnic groups. While the Act does not specifically refer to religion, it is clear that most of the religious believers covered by this guide will be members of minority ethnic groups. Some key sections are summarized below.

Section 20 makes it unlawful for anyone concerned with providing goods, services, or facilities to the public to discriminate on racial grounds by refusing or deliberately omitting to provide them, or as regards their quality or the manner in which, or the terms on which, they are provided. Discrimination may be direct (less favourable treatment), or indirect (applying conditions which have a disproportionately adverse effect on a particular racial group, and which cannot be justified).

Section 71 places a duty on every local authority to make appropriate arrangements with a view to securing that its various functions are carried out with due regard to the need:

- to eliminate unlawful racial discrimination;
- to promote equality of opportunity and good relations between people of different racial groups.

Sections 37 and 38 are positive measures encouraging employees and potential employees of a particular racial group to take up training or employment where that racial group is under-represented. However, these sections do not allow positive discrimination at the point of selection.

Section 5(2)(d) allows members of particular racial groups to be appointed to posts whose holders provide persons of that racial group with personal services promoting their welfare, which can most effectively be provided by members of that same group.

Section 35 makes lawful any act done in affording persons of a particular racial group access to facilities or services to meet the special needs of persons of that group in regard to their education, training or welfare or any other ancillary benefits.

Local contacts

These enable users of the guide to gain maximum benefit from it. Contact should be made with the nearest branches of the religious communities listed. It is important to have these local points of reference, for advice and assistance, and to see how far local practice diverges from the general outline in the guide. There is space at the end of each section for local details to be included.

National contacts

Religious communities listed do not all have national structures like major Christian denominations. Where national contacts exist, they are listed. Alternatively, other relevant institutions are used. This is another reason why making contact is particularly important. Where no address is listed, the Commission for Racial Equality may be able to advise you (Elliot House, 10/12 Allington Street, London SW1E 5EH, Tel: 071–828–7022, Fax: 071–630–7605).

Training

The guide focuses on practical operational needs in serving consumers from minority ethnic religious communities. Training should concentrate on creating agency procedures and professional practice which meet these needs.

Prayer

Staff dealing with members of minority ethnic religious communities should acknowledge appropriately their awareness of needs in respect of prayer. Members of minority ethnic religious communities are usually aware of practicalities in respect of prayer, and most have established procedures to enable them to pray within the limitations of their situation. Particular points to bear in mind are mentioned in the text.

Symbols

Typical symbols associated with the different religions are included in the text. Symbols are treated differently by the different religions; in Islam for example, symbols are not objects of veneration, and are not used in worship, as the Cross would be in Christianity.

Visiting

Assumptions underlying custom and practice in visiting clients at home need reviewing when they belong to minority ethnic religious communities. Different religious festivals and religious holidays must be respected. Prayer or meditation may take place at particular times during the day. Specific areas in the home may be set aside for worship. There will be expectations about hospitality to visitors. References to these questions appear in the text.

Religious festivals

Diaries *must* be used which contain the dates of relevant holy days and festivals. This is because the calendars by which the relevant dates are calculated differ, so that feast days are rarely fixed, and cannot readily be calculated using a conventional British calendar. Brief explanations of each festival appear in the text, but exact dates can only be given for each individual year. Certain festivals can only be approximately given, because they rely on a first sighting of celestial bodies.

Death customs

Those described assume the dying person is aware of the imminent possibility of decease. If this is knowingly concealed from a dying person or their carers, it will cause grave offence, great distress, and may prevent the proper laying to rest of the deceased.

Household size

This is greater on average among minority ethnic religious communities in Britain (4.4 persons) than among the population as a whole (2.51 persons) (OPCS 1989). This can lead to unwarranted assumptions about ability of families to meet their own needs, and should not be used to rationalize low take-up of services by minority ethnic groups.

Literacy

Command of written and spoken English among members of minority ethnic religious communities born in Britain is the same as for the rest of the population. But only about half of those born abroad may be literate in any language. Therefore, agencies seeking to attract approaches from members of minority ethnic religious communities need staff fluent in the appropriate languages to deal with clients' needs, as well as translated material. This is particularly important where sensitive personal, confidential or technical issues, for example health, personal relationships, legal, or welfare rights, are involved.

Interpreters may be essential in the short term; it is the responsibility of agencies to use the positive action provisions of the Race Relations Act (1976) to recruit a multi-racial workforce with the appropriate language skills, so that non-English speakers are not denied their services. Use of relatives to interpret is never ideal. Where confidential personal matters are concerned it may prevent clients from using a service.

'They ought to learn English'

This is a response often expressed to problems of communication. Most members of minority ethnic groups are perfectly fluent in English. Members of majority ethnic groups demanding fluent English of everyone should recall that they may be expecting more of minority ethnic groups than they expect of themselves.

Speaking languages other than the mother tongue is still relatively rare in Britain. Writing languages in totally different scripts, which may start at the opposite end and opposite side of a page, and be written below the line, as opposed to above it, is still rarer.

This may often be the equivalent of asking a left-handed person to write with his right hand. Older adults particularly, may find this very difficult. The resources needed to teach English as a second language on this scale, particularly to those not literate in their first language, should not be underestimated.

Scripts
Samples of different scripts are shown in the text. Some languages are only written, and are used together with spoken dialects. Punjabi, for example, is spoken by Sikhs, but the written language is called Gurmukhi. Sylheti is the dialect spoken by many people in Britain with a Bangladeshi cultural background, but the written language is Bengali. Chinese characters are universal in China, but are spoken differently according to the regional dialect used.

Some interpreting and translating services
Avon Community Interpreting Service, Bristol	0272–428962
Birmingham	0215–237391
Dundee	0382–832434
Leeds	0532–424311
Leicestershire Social Services Interpreting and Translating Unit	0533–323232
Lothian	0315–574591
Newcastle	0912–328520
Portsmouth	0705–822251

Vietnamese Interpreters' Group, Manchester:
Minh Bui   061–202–1383
Thong Quach   061–205–6139

JUDAISM

Main languages

ENGLISH

HEBREW Jews form an integral part of our culture, and with very few exceptions use English as their first language. In Britain, Hebrew is the language of worship, rather than everyday communication, though it is widely written and spoken in Israel.

Names

Names of Jews are not structured in any way differently from the majority. Some Jews who originally had European names have Anglicized them.

Beliefs

Judaism was founded by the prophet Abraham, whose revelation of one G-d (the name is never written in full) caused him to lead his family in a search for the Promised Land. Jews are held to be the descendants of Abraham. Their struggle to reach the Promised Land is described by the prophets of the Jewish holy book, the Torah, which is also the basis of the Christian Old Testament, and much of Islam. Judaism preserves an element of ethnic identity, unlike Christianity or Islam. The creation of the State of Israel as a national home is of great significance for Jews everywhere.

Prayer

Observing Jewish men pray three times per day. For morning prayer, a prayer shawl is worn. Phylacteries (small leather boxes containing biblical texts) are also worn, except on the Sabbath or major festivals. Morning prayer may take up to 30 minutes, or longer on the Sabbath (Saturday) morning. The very religious will not take food before morning prayer. Afternoon and evening prayer take five to ten minutes. Prayers should not be interrupted unless medically necessary. Women may also wish to pray, but they do not wear shawls or phylacteries. In addition to prayers, a short blessing is said before eating, and a somewhat longer one after a meal.

Religious festivals and the Sabbath

The Sabbath falls on each Saturday. Like festival days, it commences a quarter hour before sunset on the preceding day, and terminates just after nightfall on the day itself. Judaism uses the lunar calendar, so festival days vary from year to year. Since the Sabbath commemorates the creation of the world by G-d, religious Jews may not do 'creative' work on that day. This prohibition includes phoning, writing, using electric light or equipment, travelling by car or public transport, cooking, or carrying in, into, or out of the street, unless these acts be necessary to save life. It applies on festival days also.

SUKKOT (Tabernacles) is a nine-day harvest festival, though the middle five days are treated as weekdays. It begins five days after Yom Kippur, and commemorates the 40 years the Jews spent in the wilderness after their flight from Egypt. It involves the blessing of branches of palm, myrtle, willow and a special kind of citrus. Families at home may build a temporary hut roofed with branches and decorated with fruit, in which meals and family activities take place during the festival.

SIMCHAT TORAH immediately follows Sukkot, and celebrates the end of one annual cycle of reading of the Torah and the beginning of another.

TU B'SHEVAT is a New Year for trees, on which trees are planted, and fruit from Israel is eaten.

PURIM celebrates the deliverance of the Jews of Persia from annihilation due to the intervention of Queen Esther. The scroll of Esther is read in the morning and the evening. It is a day for celebration, the giving of gifts between family and friends, and of charity to the poor. It is preceded by a one-day fast, commemorating the Jews' fast when they learned of the plan to destroy them.

PESACH (Passover) is an eight-day festival which marks the exodus of the Jews from slavery in Egypt. The four middle days are treated as ordinary weekdays. Nothing fermented or containing yeast may be eaten from 10 a.m. on the day before Passover to the end of the festival. Much kosher food is therefore unacceptable during

Passover, and special Passover meals need to be provided.

YOM HASHOA is a Day of Remembrance for victims of the Nazi Holocaust, marked by special services and the lighting of memorial candles.

YOM HA'ATZMA'UT marks the founding of the State of Israel, by special prayers in the syna-gogue as well as other celebrations.

LAG B'OMER Omer is the period of 49 days between Passover and Pentecost. Lag B'Omer is the 33rd day, celebrating the end of a plague in Roman times, and is the only day during Omer when weddings can be performed.

SHAVUOT (Pentecost) celebrates the revelation of the Torah on Mount Sinai, and the wheat har-vest.

TISHA B'AV (The Ninth of Av) is a fast day, mourning the destruction of the First and Second Temples in Jerusalem.

ROSH HASHANAH (New Year's Day) celebrates the anniversary of the creation of the world, marking the beginning of ten days when Jews are each judged by G-d.

YOM KIPPUR (Day of Atonement) marks the end of the ten days of judgement.

HANUKKAH celebrates the re-dedication of the Temple by the Macabees. An eight-branched candlestick is used to celebrate the eight evenings of the festival; one candle is lit the first evening, two the second, and so on.

Dress

Observant Jewish men cover their heads at all times, usually with a small skull-cap, and may also wear a tasselled garment, a Tzitzith. Married Jewish women also cover their hair. Some observant Jews wear a beard throughout the year, and may also have sidelocks. During various periods in the religious calendar, Jews may not shave at all.

Diet

Kosher food should be provided, unless consumption of non-kosher food is specifically required for health reasons; in case of doubt, it is better to consult a rabbi where this is feasible. Pigs, rabbits, and birds of prey are not kosher; kosher species must be correctly slaughtered and prepared in order to remain kosher; animal products from non-kosher species may not be eaten. Fish without fins and scales may not be eaten, including all shellfish, or by-products of such fish. Meat and milk may not be eaten together, and custom may decree a gap of between one and six hours between the consumption of food containing meat and that containing milk.

All fruit and vegetables are kosher, but only cheese produced under rabbinical supervision may be eaten. Kosher food may only be prepared with dishes, utensils, cookers and equipment reserved for kosher food. This infers that manufactured food, unless prepared under rabbinical supervision, is highly unlikely to be kosher.

Any meat not specifically prepared under rabbinical supervision should be avoided. If a kosher meal cannot be provided, a vegetarian meal is preferable. If this cannot be provided, a fish meal is preferable to a meat meal. Tinned kosher species such as sardines or salmon are perfectly acceptable.

The Kashruth Guide, produced annually by the United Synagogue (Woburn House, Upper Woburn Place, London WC1H 9HP), lists products suitable for a kosher diet, whether or not they are prepared under rabbinical supervision. Where those in hospital require a stricter kosher diet than can be provided, they may wish food to be brought in for them, for which limited separate storage may be required, though pre-packed meals are available.

Fasting is required on certain days (see *Religious festivals* above); anyone whose health would be prejudiced by fasting is exempt.

Medical treatment

There are religious guidelines governing abortion, organ transplantation and donation, fertility treatment, and contraception. Apart from these, all treatment necessary to save life, particularly in

7

an emergency, should be carried out without question or delay. Post-mortems are not permitted in Jewish law except in emergency, or where required under civil law. In case of queries, contact the London Beth Din (Court of the Chief Rabbi) Tel: 071–387–5772, if no local source of advice is available.

Social customs

Modesty is very important; according to Jewish law, children should be educated in single sex schools after 11 years of age. Women should be dressed modestly, with sleeves extending to below the elbow, and hemlines to below the knee. Jewish patients should not be admitted to unisex wards.

Birth customs

Childbirth is always considered a life-threatening situation. From the point at which the mother cannot walk unaided, or begins to bleed, or have regular contractions, until thirty days after the birth, she may have whatever medical treatment may be required. Pregnancy may be terminated during childbirth up to the point when the head has been delivered, if this is necessary to save the mother's life.

After the point at which the head is delivered, the foetus is considered a separate human being, whose life may not be sacrificed, even to save the mother's life. Mothers are excused participation in any traditional fasts which may be happening

8

around the time of their confinement, for seven days from the onset of childbirth. Until the 30th day, they are only expected to fast on Yom Kippur (provided they are well). They may choose to fast on other traditional days if they are well.

Circumcision of boys called 'Bris', is carried out by a Mohel, a trained Jewish practitioner, during daylight on the eighth day after birth, even if the eighth day is the Sabbath or a festival. The day of birth is counted as the first day, unless the baby is born after nightfall. It is customary to have ten men present during the ceremony, and to have a small celebration (a meal or refreshments) afterwards. The Mohel will delay the circumcision unless the child is completely well, and may wish to see the baby several times in the first few days after the birth. The address of the local Mohel may be obtained from the Secretary of the Initiation Society, Tel: 081–203–1352.

A ceremony called 'Pidyon Ha'ben' takes place 30 days after the birth of a first-born baby boy, unless the mother has had a previous miscarriage or stillbirth, or the child was born by Caesarean section.

Death customs

Jews must be buried as soon as possible after death. Cremation is not permitted. Eyes should be closed and the jaw also. Hands (with fists unclenched) and feet are left in the normal position, and the body is covered with a white sheet.

Wherever possible, the body should not be left unattended; a rabbi or Jewish burial society should be contacted as soon as possible.

Visiting

There are no special prohibitions, but please arrange appointments in advance.

Local contact

In every case, the local congregation should be the first point of contact. London or other national contacts, mentioned in the text, should only be used when the nearest local contact is unknown, or not available in an emergency. Please use this space to enter the address and telephone number of your nearest synagogue:

....

....

....

....

....

....

HINDUISM

ॐ

Main languages

BENGALI is written from left to right

সংখ্যালঘু সম্প্রদায়ের প্রথা ওধর্মের একটি সংক্ষিপ্ত বিবরণী

PUNJABI is spoken and written in **GURMUKHI** script from left to right

ਸਿੱਖ ਮਜ਼ਬ ਦੇ ਰਵਾਜਾਂ ਬਾਰੇ

HINDI is written from left to right

कम गिनती वाले धर्मों के रीति रिवाजो
के बारे मे अल्प सूचना देने वाली पुस्तक

GUJERATI is written from left to right

અલ્પ એવી સંસ્થાના ધાર્મિક રિવાજને
ટૂંકી માર્ગદર્શિ.

Names

Hindus usually have three names; a personal name first, a complementary name (which may be joined with the first name), and lastly a family, or subcaste, name. For example Suresh Kumar Joshi is a typical Hindu man's name, or Pramilla Bala Sood for a woman. Gujerati men use their father's personal name, plus a suffix (-chand), as their middle name. Traditionally, Hindu women taken their husband's family name upon marriage. Use the family name for record purposes as a surname. Many families omit the middle name when registering the birth of a child in this country. The first letter of a child's name is decided by a priest according to the time and date of the birth. Consulting relatives and holy books may delay the naming of a baby for up to 40 days. During the interval, the baby should be known by the mother's name.

Beliefs

Hinduism is the most ancient of the world's religions. An exact date of origin is difficult to determine, since it is not based on the teachings of any one sage or prophet. Hindus believe in one divine conscious power, superior to man, manifested in many forms, with many names. These reflect different functions and attributes, but are believed by Vedic Hindus to be indivisible manifestations of one God, from whom the whole universe emanates.

God is symbolized by the word Om or Aum, where A stands for the power of God to create the universe, manifested in the form of Brahma, the Generator. U stands for the power of God to preserve the universe, manifested in the form of Vishnu, the Preserver. M stands for the power of God to dissolve or destroy the universe, manifested in the form of Rudra or Shiva, the destroyer.

Hindus believe that there are ten Avtars or incarnations of God on earth. Nine of these have been born, and a tenth is yet to come. Whenever there has been a decline in religious practice, an Avtar appears to protect the people, and punish the forces of evil. Vishnu appeared on earth as Rama, the son of King Dasratha Rama. The Ramayana, one of the Hindu holy books, tells how Rama and his consort, Sita were banished to the forest for 14 years, by his brothers, who wished to prevent his succession to the throne; Ravanna was a wicked king who kidnapped Sita; the object of the Rama Avtar was to destroy the wicked Ravanna. Krishna appeared on earth as the eighth Avtar to destroy the power of the kings of the time, and the demons.

There are five main principles of Hinduism known as the five Ps: Parmeshwar (God); Prarthana (prayer); Punarjanma (rebirth); Purushartha (law of action); Prani Daya (compassion for all living things). The four objectives set out in the Purushartha are known as: Dharma (religious duties), Artha (material prosperity), Kama (satisfaction of desire) and Moksha (salvation).

Hindu holy books include the four Vedas, the Upanishads, and the epics, from which come the Ramayana and the Bhagavad Ghita. Hindus believe they have an eternal soul – Atman. There is a strong belief in Karma, a moral law of cause and effect, which relates to the form in which a person may be reborne. Living a dutiful and virtuous life – Dharma – releases the soul from the cycle of death and rebirth.

Life is seen as having four stages: up to 25 years of age, Bramchari (student); 26 to 50 years of age, Grihastha (householder); 51 to 75 years of age,

Vanaprastha (retirement); 76 years of age onwards, Sanyasi (renunciation).

According to the Vedas, there is only one caste, humanity, but in practice Hindu society is broken down into four main groups:

Brahman – the priestly caste, who teach and perform religious ceremonies, and encourage others to learn religious duties.

Kshatriya – the military caste, who protect society and govern, rule and administer a country to lead a disciplined life.

Vaishya – who engage in business, trade, commerce and agriculture.

Shudra – the manual labourers.

Caste is inherited by birth; Hindus in Britain may observe the caste system, and wish to avoid dining or inter-marriage with members of other castes.

Prayer

Hindus will wish to pray twice daily. Acknowledging these needs will do much to create confidence. They will require copies of holy books, prayer beads, and may wish to burn incense where this is practicable. Simple gestures towards these needs, such as offering to draw curtains around a hospital bed to afford privacy for meditation, for example, will be much appreciated. At home, daily Pujah (worship) takes place before a shrine, sometimes in a room set aside for prayer. The temple (Mandir) is particularly used

15

for festivals and special celebrations. Horoscopes are an important part of Hindu religious belief.

Religious festivals

Festivals play an important role in creating pride in, and consciousness of, cultural traditions. Hindu festivals have a deep spiritual meaning, and serve many socially useful purposes: they bring people together in friendship and love; they increase religious devotion of all Hindus, who observe their festivals with great enthusiasm and joy. The festivals' most important purpose is to constantly remind Hindus of God, and the importance of leading a God-fearing life. Hindu festivals do not fall on the same date annually, being based upon the Panchang, the Hindu calendar, in which the calculation of months and years is based upon the movement of the moon around the earth. Rough indications of the period of the year when they usually fall are given, but advice given about diaries in the *General Notes* (p. xiv), needs to be followed.

DIVALI or DEEPAVALI is a reminder that justice brings victory. It signifies the victory of divine forces over those of evil. This is a fire festival of light, in which it is hoped that Lakshmi, the goddess of good fortunate and prosperity, will bless the people. Diwali celebrates the victory of Rama over Ravanna, and the homecoming of Rama and Sita who were banished to the forest for 14 years. Candles and lights are lit in all the houses to guide Lakshmi to the house. Most families celebrate by giving and receiving presents, and preparing special meals. Parties may also take place, and fireworks are lit. The festival signifies the victory of the light over darkness, knowledge over ignorance and goodness over evil.

HOLI is celebrated in northern and central India, and is related to the triumph of good over evil. The ancient legend is often associated with the Lord Krishna. Celebrations involve coloured water and coloured powder, which are mischievously thrown at friends and family. People meet in the home, the temple or the local community. A bonfire is usually lit, and religious songs are sung at the temple. Some people may fast for the day, until they visit the temple. In India, celebrations may last up to three days.

JANAMASHTAMI celebrates the birth of the Lord Krishna. Hindus may fast all day, until the birth of the Lord Krishna, which is celebrated at midnight. Many Hindus visit the local temple, where hymns and songs are devoted to the Lord Krishna. Some Hindus fast on the following day also. In this case they may end the day by enjoying sweets, and wearing new clothes. Many places in India organize plays and events which depict the life of the Lord Krishna, and his consort Radha.

MAHASHIVRATRI celebrates the birth of the Lord Shiva. Hindus may fast until 4 p.m., when they may attend a ceremony in the temple. Celebrations may be organized at night, and fasting the following day.

NAVARATRI is the Festival of Nine Lights leading up to Dussehra. This festival is dedicated to the Mother Goddess Durga or Amba. Hindus celebrate by dressing up and dancing around the deities for nine days.

DUSSEHRA (known as Durga Puja in Bengal) is the tenth day after Navaratri celebrations of the Mother Goddess Durga, the female principle of energy and motherhood. Presents are exchanged, and family celebrations take place.

RAKSHA BANDHAN celebrates the bond between brothers and sisters. Sisters will tie a silken thread to the right wrist of brothers or give ready made bracelets (Rakshi). Brothers will give gifts or money in return, and promise to protect their sisters during their lives. The sisters wish their brothers long life, prosperity, wealth, and good fortune throughout their lives.

RAMA NAVAMI or RAMNAVMI celebrates the birth of Rama, who is the incarnation of Vishnu, and hero of the epic poem, the Ramayana. Many Hindus fast during the day, avoiding grain, and certain vegetables. Most Hindus visit the temple, and/or pray at home. In India, effigies of Lord Ravanna may be burnt to depict the triumph of Rama in the battle in Lanka.

GANESH CHATURTHI celebrates the festival of Ganesh the god of prosperity and good fortune. Ganesh was the son of Shiva and Parvati, and is revered as the remover of obstacles. Ganesh is seen as the symbol of happiness, to whom Hindus pray before beginning any new venture, such as a journey, a wedding, or in business. Ganesh Chaturthi is particularly celebrated in central and western India.

SARASWATI PUJA is the celebration of Saraswati, goddess of learning and art.

Dress

Women wear a Sari, Shalwar (loose-fitting trousers) or Kameez (loose-fitting trouser suit), and a Chadar (long scarf covering the head), or Western dress. Girls wear knee-length dresses or trousers. Married women wear a red spot on the forehead (Bindi); sometimes they wear a red streak in the hair parting. Most men wear Western dress for work, but may wear traditional dress, Kameez or Kurta (long tunic) at home or on special occasions. Hindus should be modest about their bodies, and dress with respect and dignity. Hindu men cover themselves from waist to knee.

Diet

Hindus do not eat beef. Cow's milk is usually acceptable. Many Hindus refuse to kill animals for food, and are strictly vegetarian. They will have no contact with plates or utensils used for preparing or eating meat, and often eggs as well. Disposable plates will be necessary for their food. Tobacco and alcohol are forbidden. During traditional fasting periods, Hindus will still take hot milk, fruit, tea, and salad without salt. At the end

19

of a fast, Hindus will share 'prasad', a small quantity of food, possibly sweets, which has been offered to God in thanksgiving. Observant Hindus do not all fast on the same days, but may choose different days of the week on which to fast. For example, during the month of Sravan (July/August) when it is usual to do good deeds, many Hindus will abstain from eating grain, but the days upon which they do this will vary, some abstaining completely while others only on particular chosen days.

Medical treatment

Hindu women much prefer to be treated by female staff, particularly where questions of modesty are concerned. There are no special religious objections to blood transfusion or organ transplantation. Post-mortems are disliked but accepted.

Social customs

Hindus prefer to wash themselves with running water. Showers are preferred to baths, and bidets to the use of toilet paper. The concept of purity/impurity is important. Fire, water, earth, and air are each important purifiers on particular occasions.

Birth customs

As far as is practicable, mother and child should rest at home for 40 days after the birth, during which time the mother should not prepare food.

After 40 days, the mother takes a purifying bath. The infant's head is shaved in the first, third or fifth year. When a boy reaches the age of seven a sacred thread ceremony may be performed, as a reminder of his religious duties.

Death customs

Dying Hindus may be comforted by readings from holy books and the Bhagavad Ghita. They may prefer to lie on the floor, to be closer to Mother Earth. The family may wish a Hindu priest to tie a sacred thread (Yagyopavit) around the patient's wrist or neck, as a blessing, sprinkle Ganga Jal (holy Ganges water) over the patient, or place a sacred tulsi leaf or drops of Ghee (clarified butter) in the patient's mouth. Where there is no family, the patient may wish the nearest temple to be approached.

Relatives may wish to bring clothes and money for the patient to touch, before distribution to the needy; if they cannot do this themselves, they may wish a health worker to do this for them. *All possible steps should be taken to permit a Hindu to die at home, since death in hospital can cause great distress*. After a death, readings from the holy books take place at home for 5–7 days. Members of the family bathe and prepare the body for cremation, which should take place within 24 hours of death. Ashes may be scattered in any flowing river, preferably the Ganges. The family remain indoors for 10–13 days of mourning, during which any outside matters are dealt with by relatives and friends.

Visiting

When arranging to visit a Hindu household, remember that Hindus usually pray after bathing in the morning. Hindus of working age will rise early for this purpose, but older people may rise later; they will not allow visits to interrupt their morning prayer. They may also wish to meditate around midday. It is important to bear in mind the times of Hindu festivals, both when arranging visits, and also if visiting is essential at such times. It may give offence if food or drink offered to a visitor is refused without explanation. It is good to eat or drink something, if only a little.

Local contact

Please use this space to enter the name, address and telephone number of your nearest Mandir (temple) or Vedic Society:

....

....

....

....

....

....

ISLAM

Main languages

BENGALI is written from left to right, below the line

সংখ্যালঘু সম্প্রদায়ের প্রথা ও ধর্মের একটি সংক্ষিপ্ত বিবরণী

SYLHETI is spoken only

ARABIC is written from right to left

" الدليل الموجز الى المراسم الدينية للاقلية النسلية "

URDU is written from right to left

" نسل اقليت کے مذہبی مراسم کا مختصر راہنما "

Islam is a multiracial faith, and all languages may be found to some extent among Muslims.

Names

Muslims have a personal name, a name with religious or cultural significance (for example Muhammad, Abdul, Rahman, Ali, Sayed, Khan, Sheikh or -Uddin (suffix) for men, Bibi, Begum, Khatun, or Nessa for women), but not always a family name. Muslims do not usually adopt their father's, or their husband's name. Where possible, a family name should be recorded; if there is no family name, a means to identify members of one family may need to be agreed with all parties.

Muslims use different types of names; some will

24

wish to use the Muslim style, others may adopt a Western title, for example Mr, Mrs, others may adopt a Western first name. Muslim names may originate in a particular social role; for example, Sayed, Khan, or Sheikh were originally associated with leadership, and in some case still are. Choudhury is associated with the ownership of land. Begum or Bibi mean queen or princess. It is important to ask people what they want to be called.

It may take up to 21 days to name a baby; whilst waiting, the baby should be identified by the mother's name.

Beliefs

Muslims believe in one God; they accept all prophets and their books, but recognize the Prophet Muhammad (PBUH) as the latest prophet. (His name is always followed by the words 'Peace be upon him', or 'PBUH'.) Islam is a belief intended for everyone; it recognizes no caste system, and requires adherents to pray five times each day, to fast from dawn to sunset for one month each year, to give $2\frac{1}{2}$ per cent of their savings to the needy (Zakath), and to make a pilgrimage to Mecca once during their lifetime, if physically and financially able to do so. Muslims fast from dawn to sunset during the month of Ramadan. Muslims are excused fasting during sickness. Children do not fast fully until puberty. Very elderly people and children are also exempted. The Koran or Qur'ān is the holy book of Islam.

Prayer

Muslims pray five times per day (see *Visiting* below); children are encouraged to pray from the age of eight; prayer is obligatory from the age of twelve. Muslims pray facing Mecca (south-east); it will be helpful if the direction of Mecca can be simply indicated to them. (Many devout Muslims carry a compass for this purpose.) Privacy should be offered, if possible, for the purpose of prayer. Muslims in hospital may appreciate being able to have bed curtains drawn, for example. If they are bedfast, and unable physically to face Mecca, the direction should be shown to them, so that they are aware of it during prayer. Muslims would prefer to have a room set aside for prayer in a school, hospital, or workplace. Provision should be incorporated in the design of any new buildings to be used by Muslims. Wherever possible, Muslims should wash hands, face, and feet in running water before prayer. This means that it would be desirable to have toilet facilities incorporating a bidet, or another facility where feet can be washed in running water.

Religious festivals

The dates of Muslim festivals are calculated by a lunar calendar. Where a festival is fixed, the lunar date is listed.

AL HIJRAH commemorates the migration of the Prophet from Mecca to Medina. The Muslim calendar starts on the day of the Prophet's migration, AH being the equivalent of AD in the

Christian calendar, but as a lunar calendar is being used, the numbers of years are not exactly equivalent.

ASHURA commemorates the defeat and death of Hussain, son of Ali, grandson of the Prophet. Shia Muslims fast, mourn, and re-enact the events leading to his death. Sunni Muslims emulate the Prophets own fast on this day.

MUHARRAM (New Year) 1st day of the 1st lunar month.

MUHAMMAD'S BIRTHDAY 12th day of the 3rd lunar month.

LAILAT AL MIRAJ 27th night of the 7th lunar month marks the Prophet's ascent to the Throne of God above the seven skies to receive direct messages for the guidance of humankind. This is the origin of the injunction to pray five times each day.

LAILAT UL BARA'H 15th night of the 8th lunar month. Throughout this night, prayers are said for a better life, for better fortune, and for the betterment of all.

RAMADAN the 9th lunar month. This is a period of fasting during which Muslims practice self-discipline, in order to achieve tolerance, love, sacrifice and equality, by desisting between dawn and dusk from eating, quarrelling, or sexual activity. They break their fast by special meals at dawn and dusk. When Ramadan falls during the winter months, Muslims may be permitted one meal during the day. Schools should permit Muslim children exemption from physical exercise during Ramadan.

LAILAT UL QADR 27th night of the 9th lunar month. This is the night upon which the completion of the Koran is celebrated, and is considered to be the equivalent of 1 000 nights of worship. Prayers are said throughout the night, either at the mosque, or at home in addition to the reading of the Koran, which continues throughout Ramadan.

EID UL FITR 1st day of the 10th lunar month. This is the day upon which the end of Ramadan is celebrated. Special prayers are said, often in the open air in countries where the Muslim faith is predominant, preferably in a dedicated open space called an Eidgah, but usually in the mosque in Britain. Family members exchange gifts to celebrate this special feast.

HAJ 8th to 13th day of the 12th lunar month. This is an international Muslim festival, which should be celebrated once in the lifetime of each Muslim in Mecca. When a Muslim in Britain makes a pilgrimage to Mecca for Haj, an absence of at least three weeks should be expected.

EID UL ADHA 10th day of the 12th lunar month. The testing of Abraham and Ismail by God is commemorated with special prayers and the exchange of gifts. Meat from an animal ritually slaughtered (Halal) is shared between the family and the poor.

Dress

Muslims follow a code of strict modesty. Men must be covered from the navel to the knee; only the face and hands of women should be visible. Girls after puberty should have the right to practise strict modesty, for example, by covering their heads or wearing a veil, in any public environment, such as a school, college, or workplace.

Diet

No alcohol, tobacco, or drugs other than medicinal are allowed. Meat must be ritually slaughtered, (Halal). Pork, animal fats, or meat from any carnivorous animal, are forbidden. Cooking of Halal food should be with separate utensils. Halal food should not be stored or cooked with non-Halal food. All employers providing dining facilities, schools and colleges, hospitals, and residential establishments of all types, including prisons, must provide Halal food if they provide services to Muslims.

Medical treatment

Treatment by a medical attendant of the same sex is strongly preferred. Post-mortems are only permitted when legally required. There are no other specific religious prohibitions.

Social customs

Sexual segregation (Purdah) may be enforced after puberty, and is encouraged in the years leading up to puberty. Single sex education must be provided. The sexes must be segregated in any activity where the body is only partly covered, for example swimming. Sexual relations before marriage are totally prohibited. Mothers giving birth outside marriage are liable to be rejected by their community.

Birth customs

The Azan (call to prayer) is recited after the birth.

Death customs

A dying Muslim should be turned to face Mecca (south-east). Other Muslims, preferably the family, comfort the dying patient with prayers, and by reciting the passages from the Koran for peace of the soul. After death, because the body is the property of Allah, it must be in the custody of Muslims. Should non-Muslims be required to touch the body, they should wear disposable gloves.

Washing and preparation of bodies for burial should be carried out by Muslims. After washing, the body is dressed in a white shroud, called a Kaffon, and prayers are said. The body must be buried in a Muslim cemetery, within 24 hours of death. The anniversary of a death is commemorated in a family by the giving of alms, on the basis that the living must undertake the obligations which the dead person is no longer able to fulfil.

Visiting

An appointment should avoid the times of daily prayer; these are at dawn, just after midday, halfway between noon and sunset, at sunset, and one-and-a-half hours after sunset. Precise times vary with the calendar. If a room in a Muslim house is reserved for prayer, shoes should not be worn in that room. It is important to avoid visiting during Muslim festivals.

Local contact

Please use this space to enter the address and telephone number of your nearest mosque; enquiries should be addressed to the Imam:

....

....

....

....

....

....

SIKHISM

Main language

PUNJABI is the spoken language

GURMUKHI is the script in which Punjabi is written. It is written from left to right.

ਸਿੱਖ ਮਜ਼ਬ ਦੇ ਰਵਾਜਾਂ ਬਾਰੇ

Names

Sikhs have a personal name, a title, Singh (lion) for men, or Kaur (princess) for women, and a family name. For example Bhupinder Singh Gill. Sikh personal names are unisex, hence it is essential to use the title Singh or Kaur when wishing to denote gender. Sikhs may prefer to be addressed by their personal name and title, but the family name should be used for record purposes; for example B.S. Gill. Women adopt their husband's family name on marriage.

Beliefs

Sikhism originated in the Punjab in the 15th century in the teachings of Guru Nanak, combining aspects of Hinduism and Islam. Guru Nanak and his nine successors are revered as saints, whose collected writings form the Sikh holy book, the Guru Granth Sahib. Sikhs have an individual relationship with one God, with whom they aim to achieve unity through cycles of death and rebirth. Sikhs may be Saihajdhari (apprentices in

Sikhism), or Amritdhari (baptized). Amritdhari observe strict rules of diet, dress, prayer and worship at the temple. Sikhs reject the caste system, believing that people should be treated equally.

Prayer

Sikh morning prayer, Japji, takes place either before or after sunrise, and evening prayer, Rehras, either before or after sunset. There are no set times for prayer in the sense that missing a time of prayer is considered a sin. Sikhs are asked to keep repeating the hymns whenever they find time. Because precise times of prayer vary, tactful enquiry should be made when arranging to visit a household. Sikh homes may have a shrine where the Guru Granth Sahib is reserved. Where this is in an area set aside for prayer, shoes should not be worn in this area, and the head should be covered. This also applies in visits to Sikh temples. Alcohol and tobacco are forbidden within the premises of a shrine. One should not visit a temple if alcohol has recently been consumed.

Religious festivals

There are major Sikh festivals on 13/14 January, on 13 April (Vasakhi) and a third feast, Diwali, which is movable. Vasakhi is preceded by three days of prayer, and commemorates the founding of the Sikh Order of Khalsa (into which Amritdhari are baptized), by Guru Gobind Singh.

MARTYRDOM OF GURU ARJAN DEV commemorates the death by torture of the fifth guru, in 1606. Guru Arjan Dev compiled the Guru Granth Sahib, and oversaw the completing of the Golden Temple of Amritsar.

BIRTHDAY OF GURU NANAK is celebrated by 'Akhand Path', a complete reading of the Guru Granth Sahib, begun two days before the Birthday, in order to finish on the morning of the Birthday itself. Sikhs gather at the Gurdwara (temple) where hymns and sermons celebrate the life and work of Guru Nanak, and food from the free kitchen is shared among the congregation.

MARTYRDOM OF GURU TEGH BAHADUR commemorates the public execution of the ninth guru by order of the Moghul emperor in 1675.

BIRTHDAY OF GURU GOBIND SINGH is also celebrated by 'Akhand Path', as with Guru Nanak.

Ceremonies are relatively few in the Sikh religion, apart from the above and the celebration of weddings and baptisms.

Dress

Amritdhari observe the 5 Ks. Cutting of hair is forbidden (Kesh); the hair is secured with a comb (Khanga); the head is always covered, the man's with the turban. A metal bangle is worn on the right wrist (Kara), and a small symbolic dagger (Kirpan). Men wear short underbreeches (Kachha). Saihajdhari assume aspects of this dress, according to the stage in their progress towards Amrit (baptism). *The 5 Ks are sacred, and should not be disturbed unless absolutely necessary.*

Diet

Dairy products are important. *Beef is forbidden.* Many Sikhs are vegetarian, and should be told the contents of dishes where this is not obvious. No alcohol or tobacco is permitted. Sikhs may fast if they feel it to be beneficial to their health, but their religion does not require it. In communities with a large enough Sikh population to support specialist butchers, Sikhs eat meat slaughtered according to a special rite, called Chakard or Chattaka (there may be other regional vernacular forms of this word). They will not eat Halal meat. Chicken, lamb or pork are preferred.

Medical treatment

There is no religious objection to blood transfusion, organ transplantation, or post-mortem examination. Sikh women will wish to see a female doctor; modesty is of great importance to them.

Social customs

Sikh men may be gravely embarrassed if required to remove their Kachha or turban; tactful explanation if this becomes absolutely necessary will be greatly appreciated. If a school uniform is worn, parents may not permit girls to wear a skirt, and in this case will provide Shalwar (loose-fitting trousers) of the correct colour. Similarly, parents may require that girls be allowed to wear track-suits for PE. After the age of 12, swimming may not be permitted for girls. Sikhs believe in the dignity of labour and are always ready to accept whatever work they may find. Baptized Sikhs will refuse to accept work which requires them to remove their turban or shave off their hair.

Birth customs

Births are celebrated by thanksgiving at the Gurdwara (temple). At 13 days, the baby may be baptized into the Order of Khalsa. Baptism is administered by five Sikhs in the presence of the holy book, and may be performed at home or in the temple. At the first feast of Vasakhi, (Spring Festival and New Year on 13 April) after the birth, the 5 Ks become obligatory for baptized Sikhs. Mothers are forbidden to prepare food for 40 days after the birth, and are encouraged to rest. Mothers are given rich food after the birth. Sweets are distributed to celebrate the birth of a boy. Many girls have their ears pierced at an early age.

Death customs

A dying Sikh will be comforted by reciting hymns from the Guru Granth Sahib. If the patient is too ill to recite, then a relative or a Granthi (reader) from the local temple may do so. Should neither be available, the patient may ask any practising Sikh to do so. The body may usually be tended by non-Sikhs, who may perform the last offices if the family so wishes. *The family is responsible for all ceremonies and rites at death, and must be asked if they wish to wash and lay out the body themselves.* If there is no family, the nearest Sikh temple must be consulted. Sikhs are always cremated, and their ashes should be scattered in running water, preferably the Ganges. In Britain, rivers, seas or lakes are treated as running water.

Mourning varies in length; a long and full life, with many offspring, grandchildren, and great-grandchildren, may be a cause for celebration. A premature death will be likely to call for a period of full mourning. Funeral rites, with a procession to the crematorium, are of great social significance. When attending funerals, women should wear a white head covering.

Visiting

Visiting should be avoided during times of prayer or festival days. It is important to respect areas in a home which are set aside for prayer. If refreshment is offered in a Sikh home, offence may be caused if this is refused without explanation.

Local contact

Please use this space to enter the address and telephone number of your nearest Gurdwara (temple); enquiries should be addressed to the Temple President:

....

....

....

....

....

....

BUDDHISM AND REVERENCE FOR ANCESTORS VIETNAMESE

Editor's Note: There is a distinctive community of Chinese descent throughout Vietnam, sometimes resident for many generations, which has nonetheless retained its distinctive culture and customs. These may more typically be described in the section on Buddhism/Taoism/Confucianism. Among Vietnamese in Britain *not* of Chinese descent, Reverence for Ancestors is likely to be combined with Buddhism, though many Vietnamese in Britain are Roman Catholic. Though there are significant common aspects of the two cultures, Vietnamese not of Chinese descent may wish to emphasize their distinct cultural identity.

Main language

VIETNAMESE is a tonal language of short syllables; different tonal emphasis conveys different meaning. It is written in a modified Latin alphabet. The accents above or below words indicate the tone.

Chỉ Nam Giản Lược Về Phong Tục Và

Tôn Giáo Của Các Giống Dân Thiểu Số

Names

Vietnamese names have three parts: a family name, a complementary name, and a personal name. Some Vietnamese in Britain reverse this traditional order, giving family name last. If in doubt, ask for the family name. Vietnamese people share about 25 different family names. One of the most common is Nguyen. The complementary name Van is often used for men, and Thi for women. Personal names of men and women tend to associate them with traditional male or female qualities, but often it is not possible to determine sex from a given individual name. Married women do not adopt their husband's family name.

Beliefs

Reverence for Ancestors is very important to Vietnamese people, and this may also extend to national heroes and heroines. A second main philosophy influencing daily life is Buddhism. Buddhism sees life as a process of birth, ageing, illness and death, in which people achieve enlightenment by suffering and overcoming grief. Roman Catholicism is also important among Vietnamese in Britain; there are examples of whole Catholic congregations seeking refuge in Britain.

Some families hold to not only one belief, but a mixture of two, or parts of all three are quite usual. In Buddhist and Catholic families, a family shrine dedicated to ancestors is usual, often featuring photographs of recently deceased relatives. Incense sticks are a feature of domestic shrines, which are usually on shelves, painted brown or red, wide enough for food to be placed on the shrine for ceremonial occasions. There is a special emphasis on family life and the extended family, both socially and in terms of beliefs.

Beliefs and social rules are more closely inter-twined than in Western countries.

Prayer

Set forms of prayer are only used by Catholic families.

Religious festivals

TET is Vietnamese New Year. Celebrated by the extended family, it is a time for presents, new clothes, feast meals, and gifts of money to all young children.

MOON FESTIVAL is a celebration of the new moon which is usually in late August or early September. The festival is not universally celebrated, for instance it is not as widely observed in Britain as it would be by Vietnamese living in France.

Dress

Western dress is usually worn. Traditional dress, the Ao Dai, may be worn on special occasions, such as Tet, Moon Festival, weddings and engagements. This is a high-necked close-fitting garment, with a side slit, mainly worn by women from the south of Vietnam. There is a male equivalent, but this is now rarely seen.

Diet

Buddhists may have vegetarian days each

month. Nearly every dish has vegetables and herbs, similar in appearance to Chinese food, but with less use of oil. Lamb is not eaten, and there is an emphasis on fish, shellfish, poultry and pork. Fish sauce is regularly used.

Medical treatment

In Vietnam, appointments are not usually made for medical attention. Vietnamese people may require explanation of the processes of registering with a GP, and requesting home visits. There is widespread use of herbal medicine, acupuncture and massage.

Social customs

Traditional Vietnamese society reflected the Confucian idea of Ming, meaning 'name', and Fen, meaning 'duty'. The name confers status upon the individual, defining his/her role in the hierarchy of family, and clan. The three-generational household is the most important social unit in Vietnam, upon which the care of the sick, the young, the old and the poor, depend. These family ties are extremely strong and significant for Vietnamese people. They help explain the extreme sense of loss felt by many Vietnamese in Britain, particularly those who came here alone.

Birth customs

Mother and baby stay at home for the first month after the birth. At the end of this period a special meal is prepared, to which friends and relatives are invited to celebrate the new arrival.

Death customs

When a member of a family dies, the body is usually kept at home for one to three days. During this time, friends and relatives come to pay their respects with offerings of money or food. On the day of the funeral, the coffin is carried in procession to the grave, and often a priest or Buddhist monk is invited to come, to pray for the soul of the dead person. Most Vietnamese homes have altars dedicated to family ancestors. After a death, the family altar is wrapped in a white cloth for one month. On each anniversary of a death, an offering of food is made to show respect and honour the memory of the deceased relative. Dishes are ritually placed on the altar, and later eaten at a special family gathering.

National contact

Vietnam Refugee National Council
Hughes Field Community Centre
New King Street
Deptford
London SE8 3HU
Tel: 081–691–5181

Ockendon Venture
Tel: 0483–772012

Nguyen Ninh Quang An Tu
240a Clapham Road
Stockwell
London SW9 0PZ

Local contact

Please use this space to enter the name, address
and telephone number of your nearest contact:

....

....

....

....

....

....

BUDDHISM, TAOISM AND CONFUCIANISM: CHINESE

Main languages

MANDARIN

少 數 民 族 宗 教 的 風 俗 簡 介

Chinese people share a written pictorial language of some 16 000 characters, each standing for an entire word. Characters are traditionally written in vertical columns, starting in the top right hand corner, and reading from top to bottom. In contemporary Britain, this is often changed to read from left to right horizontally, as in the example above. The sound associated with each character differs according to the regional dialect spoken. About 3 000 of these 16 000 characters are in common use. Leaflets and forms translated into Chinese characters can be read by any literate Chinese, regardless of spoken dialect. Of the many regional dialects, Cantonese and Hakka are most frequently found in Britain.

Names

Chinese names often consist of three Chinese characters, though examples of two or even four may be found. Traditionally, the family name comes first, then personal names. While the names should strictly be translated separately, Chinese people may run two personal names into one. For example: Wong May Lin, Wong being the family name, and May Lin, (or Maylin) the personal name. Married women add the husband's family name as a prefix. If Wong May Lin married Mr Chang, she would become Chang Wong May Lin.

Common Chinese family names are Chang, Lee, Wong, Ho and Cheung. Some Chinese people add an English personal name, in which case they will usually put the family name last. There are variations in practice, in which married women retain their maiden name, or relinquish their maiden name and adopt their husband's name. In the former case, children will take the father's family name. If in doubt, ask which is the family name.

Beliefs

Chinese people are likely to be influenced by a variety of beliefs. Buddhism, Confucianism, and Taoism are all likely to figure in bringing up a Chinese child. Ancestor worship is also still very strong in the Chinese belief system. In converting Chinese people to Christianity, efforts were made to discourage these ideas, but their influence is all-pervasive. However, these ideas may not be so strong in those brought up on the mainland of China, particularly people born since the Second World War.

BUDDHISM sees life as a process of birth, ageing, illness and death, in which people achieve en-lightenment by suffering and overcoming grief.

TAOISM sees life as composed of a balance of fire, water, earth, metal and wood. Illness occurs when there is an imbalance in these elements, which traditional treatment seeks to restore.

CONFUCIANISM is an ethical system emphasizing respect for authority, seeing law as essential in order to make life possible. The emphasis on law and learning places teachers in particularly high esteem.

Prayer

Shrines are not usually found in Chinese homes, though altars may be set up temporarily for specific festivals or weddings. Chinese born since the Second World War often need to seek guidance from older relatives when preparing altars for specific events, such as weddings.

Religious festivals

CHING MING is a family festival, where family graves are visited. After these are cleaned and swept, families often picnic beside the graves, to share the meal with their ancestors.

CHUNG YUAN is a Buddhist festival when objects for use in the spirit world are made and offered to assist spirits with no descendants or resting place, to reach Nirvana. Large paper boats are made and burnt at temples. This festival is less often celebrated in Britain.

DRAGON BOAT FESTIVAL commemorates the suicide by drowning of the poet and statesman

Ch'u Yuan. It is marked by dragon boat racing and picnics on or near to rivers. Sweet or savoury rice balls wrapped in leaves, called Jong, are eaten.

YUAN TAN (Chinese New Year) is celebrated on the first day of the first lunar month, with fireworks, dancing, and the giving of gifts, sweets, and flowers. Gold symbolizes prosperity and red symbolizes good luck. Celebrations can last more than three days. All debts should be settled before New Year begins.

TENG CHIEH (Lantern Festival) marks the first full moon of the year, and the lengthening of the days. Homes will be decorated with strings of lanterns. This is now less often celebrated than the early autumn Moon Festival, which is celebrated with lanterns, moon cakes, and fruits.

Dress

Chinese people in Britain predominantly wear Western dress.

Diet

There are few dietary taboos, though there may be a preference for Chinese cuisine. Diet may be influenced by Chinese cultural beliefs about health being related to a balance of physical elements in the body (see *Taoism* above). A Chinese person may feel that cold food should not be eaten by a sick person, or that a certain condition indicates a need to alter diet in a particular way.

Medical treatment

Chinese medicine is a well-established body of holistic ideas, in accord with widespread cultural attitudes, particularly of Taoism and Buddhism. While these are different from the technical rationale of Western medicine, the attitudes involved, such as the need to tolerate suffering in order to attain enlightenment (Buddhism) and respect for authority and scholarly attainment (Confucianism), help a Chinese patient to cope with illness, and accept treatment in a disciplined manner. Herbal preparations and acupuncture are often used. Preference for Western or traditional medicine will vary with upbringing and age group.

Social customs

Chinese society involves little emotional display or physical contact, even between parents and children. Expressions of loyalty and affection are more likely to be practical, for example gifts. Brides are traditionally dressed in red, though the Western fashion for the white wedding dress is gaining strength.

Respect for elders is widely shown; for example, a daughter would not be so familiar as to address her mother's friends by their names, instead they would be addressed as 'aunty' or 'uncle'. A friend of an elder sibling would be addressed as 'older brother' or 'older sister'. A person's family of origin is of great significance; hence the retention of the maiden name by many married women. Fong Sui, which literally translated means 'wind and water', refers to the feeling or ambience associated with a place. It is important to establish good Fong Sui, and Chinese people may go to quite elaborate lengths to achieve this. This may involve the style or character or location of a building, for example.

Efforts are sometimes made to suppress left-handedness in children. This is a matter of social conformity, rather than a specific taboo. For example, Chinese people traditionally use the right hand to hold chopsticks, left-handed people might tend to clash with their neighbours at the table.

Birth customs

Boys are often favoured over girls. They are traditionally seen as the bearers of the family name and predominant heirs to family property. Fathers are rarely present at a birth. Relatives mark a birth by giving money in red envelopes. There is a special celebration called Mun Yui to mark the first month of life.

Death customs

White is the colour of mourning. As there is major emphasis on family life, a person should die in the presence of relatives, preferably at home. If possible, a Chinese person will wish to return to the community of their birth to die. To die alone, or without issue, is considered a very sad fate for a Chinese person.

Visiting

When visiting socially, Chinese people usually bring a small gift, such as fruit, sweets or cakes.

Local contact

Please use this space to enter the name, address and telephone number of your nearest contact:

....

....

....

....

....

....

RASTAFARIANISM

Editor's Note: Rastafarianism reflects a search for identity by black people who have been uprooted from their African past, and experienced a further assault on their cultural traditions in a move from the Caribbean to Britain. This latter move has led to a divergence in Rastafarian custom and practice between Britain and the Caribbean. What is written here reflects the stricter Caribbean tradition, from which many Rastafarians in Britain will have to some extent departed.

Main language

ENGLISH Rastafarians speak English, Creole, or Patois, which is a mixture of English, African, and other European languages. The form of speech varies widely in custom and practice. Distinctive words and phrases are used, for example 'Irie', a form of greeting, recognition or approval, or 'I and I', which may mean 'I' singular or plural, depending on the situation. The language style is called Iritical, combining the words 'spiritual' and 'critical'. Rastafarian language is critical of English, describing it as the language of the 'downpresser'. Semantic association of words is important.

Names

English or Africanized English names are used. Old Testament names are preferred, for example Reuben, Simeon or Levi, because Rastafarians have an Afrocentric interpretation of the Holy

Scriptures, seeing the Twelve Tribes of Israel as African people. Rastas may address one another as Rasta, Dread, or Dreaddy, when the formal name is not used. Authentic African names are also adopted, and new African-influenced names are created.

Beliefs

Rastafarians prefer the term 'principles', rather than 'beliefs', holding that the latter infer doubt. Rastafari was founded in Jamaica in the 1920s, but only took the name with the coronation of Emperor Haile Selassie of Ethiopia, in 1930. It is linked to early Christianity and Judaism. Rastafarians try to follow the Nazarite Vow of Separation, which forbids the cutting of hair, proscribes certain foods, and also requires the shunning of the dead, emphasizing life, not death.

Haile Selassie is seen as the Ras (Prince) Tafari, or Messiah. Prior to Haile Selassie's death, many Rastafarians joined the Ethiopian Orthodox Church, because the emperor was responsible for its establishment in the Caribbean. Most Rastafarians do not belong to this church, as they do not make a distinction between it and other orthodox churches.

Many Rastafarians in Britain belong to an organization known as the Twelve Tribes of Israel. They seek to educate the young to help in the advancement of black people, the liberation of Africa, and the promotion of Ethiopian and African culture. The Rastafari 'livity' (way of life) is concerned with obeying Jah's (God's) pre-flood commandments to man, the recreation of Eden through righteous living and recognition of Ethiopia as the New Jerusalem and a spiritual homeland. The Bible, including the Apocrypha, and Ethiopian history are closely studied. Obedience to the Ten Commandments of the Old Testament is recognized as being equal in importance for Rastafarians as obedience to the teachings of Jesus Christ as contained in the New Testament.

Rastafarian symbols include the Cross and the Star of David (emphasizing the Judaeo-Christian foundation of Rastafarian principles), but particularly the crowned Lion of Judah, carrying the Cross over his shoulder, from which flies the flag of Ethiopia, in red, green and gold. His Imperial Majesty Emperor Haile Selassie of Ethiopia was also entitled the Lion of Judah.

Prayer

The Rastafarian form of worship is the Nyabinghi. Reggae music was developed from the heartbeat rhythm of the Nyabinghi drums.

Religious festivals

Rastafarians celebrate Christmas on 7 January. 23 July is the birthday of Haile Selassie. Other important days include the anniversary of His Imperial Majesty's coronation, 2 November, and Marcus Garvie's birthday, 17 August. In the Caribbean, Rastafarians celebrate the anniversary of the formation of the Organisation of

African Unity (African Liberation Day) and Haile Selassie's visit to the Caribbean, around the week of 21/25 April.

Dress

Hair is worn in dreadlocks (uncut hair, washed but not brushed) and covered with a woolly hat often in the Ethiopian colours of red, green and gold (in that order) called a Tam. Rastafarian men uncover their dreadlocks during worship, but women keep their heads covered during worship, when in public or when receiving visitors. A variety of Rasta hats are called Crowns, an alternative name for a Tam. Clothing may be conventional, or more elaborate and distinctive. Khaki outfits, with sandals, or African styles are often worn. Women wrap their hair and wear colourful dresses concealing the body, as required by Rastafarian beliefs.

Diet

Most do not eat meat, but fish with scales may be acceptable. *Pork is absolutely forbidden*. Fresh natural (Ital) foods are preferred to processed food. Natural herbs and spices are liberally used. Many Rastafarians follow Jewish dietary restrictions, and will not eat grapes, currants or raisins.

Medical treatment

Herbal treatment is favoured, but conventional treatment is acceptable. Blood transfusion may be refused. Contraception is rejected, and birth control should be by self-control. Departure from this is considered a compromise, and is unlikely to be openly discussed.

Social customs

Rastafarians emphasize cultivation of land, and self-employment particularly in craft or other creative cultural activity. The principles of collective work are also important. Birthdays are not widely celebrated.

Birth customs

Natural methods of childbirth are preferred. Special herbal preparations may be given to mothers during pregnancy, labour, and after childbirth. African traditions connected with disposal of the placenta and umbilical cord, and relating to the naming of the child may be observed. A time of separation and purification may be observed after the birth.

Death customs

The Nazarite Vow enjoins the shunning of dead bodies, which may be prepared for burial by family members, or preferably an undertaker. Attendance at funerals is not emphasized, as Rastafarianism celebrates life, rather than death.

Local contact

Please use this space to enter the name, address and telephone number of your nearest contact:

....

....

....

....

....

....

Endpiece

We hope you have found the guide useful, and that you have enjoyed reading and using it. It has now grown through five locally produced editions, and this, the first Arena edition. We hope it will continue to grow through many more. As authors, we have gained much from the comments of all our users, as well as members of minority ethnic communities.

We have grown in understanding and appreciation of the issues through this contact, and hope the guide will help to share this understanding. So please write to us with your comments, be they kind or angry!

The purpose of our enterprise from the beginning has been to promote wholeness and a widening of shared understanding and mutual respect. To live in peace, with racial equality and justice, as human beings sharing a common home, has been and remains our aim. Your comments and reactions can help to realise this goal.

David Collins
Manju Tank
Abdul Basith

Note: this guide grew out of a local project in Hampshire. The guides which were originally produced were dedicated to Hampshire, containing local contact addresses, and a Foreword by the Bishop of Portsmouth. Similarly dedicated editions, containing contact addresses appropriate to a particular district or agency, and with forewords contributed by leading figures appropriate to the area or use concerned, have also been produced. Customers interested in having dedicated editions may contact the editor.

Please write to the editor:
David Collins
PDCSR
All Saints Church
Commercial Road
Portsmouth PO1 4BT